THE GIFT OF MINDFULNESS

YVETTE JANE

summersdale

THE GIFT OF MINDFULNESS

Summersdale Publishers Ltd
46 West Street
Chichester
West Sussex
PO19 1RP
UK

www.summersdale.com

Printed and bound in the Czech Republic

ISBN: 978-1-84953-605-9

Substantial discounts on bulk quantities of Summersdale books are available to corporations, professional associations and other organisations. For details contact Nicky Douglas by telephone: +44 (0) 1243 756902, fax: +44 (0) 1243 786300 or email: nicky@summersdale.com.

2018

TO......Cathé.....................................

FROM.....Margaret xo...................

Mindfulness is a means of restoring our peace and balance by bringing our wandering minds back to the present.

Do you find yourself always on the lookout for something new, different or better? Mindfulness is a reminder that you have everything in this very moment. Non-striving and acceptance are powerful allies that can strengthen what you do now, leading to contentment and fulfilment.

This book is a signpost, pointing the way towards the gift of mindfulness.

Simply sit and be still
for two minutes, bringing
your awareness to your
body and heart.

Be more awake to your day – take purposeful pauses before and after any experience or task.

In this moment, notice whether you are ruminating over the past or worrying about the future. When you find yourself caught up in a tangle of thoughts, place your hand on your heart. See if you can feel it beating and notice how your chest rises and falls with every breath. Think of all the heartbeats doing the same thing across the world, then move on with a renewed sense of shared experience.

Don't take things for granted. Your newborn nephew, family gatherings, freshly picked strawberries and the blackbird's song outside your window – all of these are moments to experience fully. They can become lifelong memories.

GET OUT OF YOUR
HEAD AND GET INTO
YOUR HEART. THINK
LESS, FEEL MORE.

Osho

The next time you're outside, let your gaze settle on a flower. Absorb every aspect of its pure bright colour and soft velvety petals, and take in its delicate fragrance.

Being busy and living
in a fast-paced manner is
a choice. Be aware that
peace and calm can be
cultivated by slowing
things down a little.

Before you leave the house, ground your awareness in your body by focussing on the connection between your feet and the earth. Slow down your breathing so that it is calm and deep, allowing your abdomen to rise and fall with every breath. Whisper to yourself, 'I am strong and grounded', then stride out with renewed strength and dignity.

If you are travelling to a new place, bring your presence and full attention to all that you experience. It is easy to get distracted by taking photographs and buying souvenirs; our minds race ahead to when we can share these things with others. Allow *yourself* plenty of moments to completely enjoy.

A BRIEF PAUSE WILL HELP YOU MAKE A SMARTER NEXT MOVE.

Peter Bergman

Cradle a mug of your favourite hot drink and savour everything about it.

When your mind is
quiet you are likely to
perceive the world with
a deeper clarity.

Every kind of sporting activity requires a good deal of focus. If you are a team player you need to keep your attention on your teammates and the game. All these opportunities are a great way to practise mindfulness and combine keeping fit with a lot of fun.

Mindful eating is a way to rediscover something that we usually take for granted. Eat something small like a peach or an apple, savouring every mouthful. The smell, taste and overall sensation of food can be a revelation when we eat slowly. Enjoy some mindful eating every day – *Bon appétit!*

JUST AS EVERY DROP OF THE OCEAN CARRIES THE TASTE OF THE OCEAN, SO DOES EVERY MOMENT CARRY THE TASTE OF ETERNITY.

Nisargadatta Maharaj

Breathing happens unconsciously, all the time. When you remember to become mindful of your breath, you bring your full awareness to the present moment. This empowers you to make a clear choice, unhindered by past influences or future anxieties.

Allow time for silence
and feel the stress receding
from your mind.

Whenever you arrive somewhere, give yourself a moment to 'check in'. Become aware of how your body is feeling – especially any aches and tensions. Take note of what emotions you are carrying. Acknowledge all of this, taking no more than a minute, and you will be centred and present, ready to move on.

Have you ever missed your turning when driving home, or found that you can't remember a thing about the day before? This can happen when our minds are brooding over past issues, planning future tasks or simply hanging out in dreamland. Up to 90 per cent of our actions arc done in this way – on automatic pilot. Bring your presence to the present and notice how vibrant life can feel.

LOOK AT A TREE, A
FLOWER, A PLANT...
ALLOW NATURE TO
TEACH YOU STILLNESS.

Eckhart Tolle

Mindfulness is seeing things with fresh eyes, with a beginner's mind rather than a jaded, world-weary sigh.

'I am peaceful and strong.' When you recite such a phrase to yourself, you reaffirm your own self-belief and strengthen the resolve in your mind.

Take a walk in a woodland or other green area and bring all your senses to the process. Be aware of your movements, the continually changing sky overhead, the mud squelching beneath your boots and the myriad of smells as they fill your nostrils. Be present with all these sensations and with the feelings that arise, as you walk in your corner of nature.

Start paying attention to things you previously overlooked. Encourage yourself to observe what a person is wearing, read a car number plate or check what colour the walls around you are. You may be astonished at the number of things you have not noticed before.

THIS IS A WONDERFUL
DAY. I'VE NEVER SEEN
THIS ONE BEFORE.

Maya Angelou

Whenever you are going out, remember to say goodbye to everyone who's present, giving them your full attention and love.

Memories – don't forget to be present and mindful while they are being made.

Before you sit down to eat as a family, light a candle and say a few words aloud to declare the intention for a happy and enjoyable meal together. All past quibbles are dissolved and the present experience can be savoured among loved ones.

Our reactions are hard-wired within us – see if you can become more aware of how you behave when you are faced with challenges. Very often our innate response happens before we have stopped to give it some thought.

THE UNIVERSE IS FULL
OF MAGIC THINGS,
PATIENTLY WAITING
FOR OUR SENSES TO
BECOME SHARPER.

Eden Phillpotts

Look around you and focus on the colours that you see. Take a full gaze and absorb the hues of purple sunsets, yellow pumpkins, ruby berries or the slate-grey sea.

As you wash your hands, give your full attention to the process of massaging the soap and warm water across your skin. Feel grateful for all the things your hands enable you to do.

There is great truth in the familiar saying, 'Don't judge a book by its cover.' Be aware of how we pre-judge people by their appearance, among other things. Being mindful means seeing everything in the present moment and not leaping to unfounded conclusions.

Make any journey pleasant by bringing your awareness to your surroundings and leaving yourself plenty of travelling time. You will arrive stress-free and alert.

THE QUIETER YOU BECOME, THE MORE YOU CAN HEAR.

Ram Dass

Mindfulness is about where you place your attention.

When you next find yourself searching in the fridge for a snack, stop and become aware of what you are feeling. Recognise that you are looking for something that you think will bring you satisfaction. Sit down and be fully present with this wanting; see how this mindfulness can relax your desire. Maybe you don't need that chocolate ice cream after all!

Make mindful choices when it comes to media overload. We can be bombarded with information from television, radio, the internet and smart phones, so be aware of how this affects you. Choose to simply switch technology off for blocks of time to allow calm to flourish.

Be mindful of your speech – pause before you reply to others and bring awareness and wisdom to your words.

MINDS ARE LIKE
PARACHUTES – THEY
ONLY FUNCTION
WHEN OPEN.

Thomas Dewar

Enjoy the gift of each moment, giving space and attention to your experiences.

Be a tourist for a day – it could even be in your own town. Bring a sense of renewal and awareness to a place you have perhaps overlooked before now.

Strong emotions, such as anger, hurt or fear, can erupt very quickly. In the split second before this happens, allow yourself to pause before you react. Become mindful of your breath and notice the sensations in your body. You then have a choice about what you do next.

Bring your full attention to the experience of having a shower or bath. Notice how the water feels and the sound it makes. Savour the scent of the soap and shampoo and be aware of the variety of textures beneath your hands. Finish by imagining that you are washed clean of negativity.

EVERYTHING PASSES,
NOTHING REMAINS.
UNDERSTAND THIS,
LOOSEN YOUR GRIP
AND FIND SERENITY.

Surya Das

Open up moments of calm throughout your day. This could be a few seconds spent in quiet stillness while the kettle boils, while your computer is switching on, or before leaving the house.

Look at something for a
moment with affection.
Soften your gaze and
bring to it the same sort of
attention as you would
a child or a baby.

When shopping for food, give some thought to the people involved in growing, packaging and transporting it. Every decision we make reverberates throughout the world, so bring awareness to the interconnections that flow through our food sources and the planet. Be a caring consumer.

A 'mindful body scan' practised regularly can be a helpful way to cope with chronic pain. Lie down and move your focus across all parts of your body, being open and curious to the sensations you find. You may feel areas of tension or discomfort; accept this while breathing slowly and calmly. For full instructions on how to perform a 'mindful body scan', search the internet or purchase a guided CD.

Mindfulness is a tool for
staying focussed.

Slow down and notice the things that make you smile.

PUT YOUR EAR DOWN
CLOSE TO YOUR SOUL
AND LISTEN HARD.

Anne Sexton

We often find that when we listen to others we are concentrating on what to say next, filling up with opinions or even speaking out of turn. Try listening with mindfulness – hear the person without judgement or the need to immediately express a view. Be aware that the word 'listen' can be shuffled around to spell 'silent'.

Observe the ordinary events that occur around you. When you spend an extra moment looking, they can transform into rich treasures. Think back to your own childhood and recall that some of the most vivid and happy memories were made when you were doing the simplest of everyday things.

THE GREAT BENEFIT
OF PRACTISING
MINDFULNESS... IS
PRESENCE OF MIND
WITHIN A STORM OF
EMOTIONS.

Phillip Moffitt

Swimming is a naturally relaxing exercise and can inspire inner quietness. Bring your complete focus to the movements of your body through the water, while setting worries to one side.

Take time to people-watch
from a cafe window with
a relaxed attention and
kind curiosity.

If you struggle to get to sleep at night, give yourself some time to unravel your stresses beforehand. Keep your laptop out of the bedroom and create surroundings that are a haven of tranquillity. Limit the stimulation of television and turn towards self-nurturing with warm drinks, relaxing baths and slow, calming music.

Practise breath awareness whenever you do something like brush your teeth or put on your socks. When we interrupt automatic behaviour, we give ourselves the chance of being in the present moment and remembering that we have choices.

Set your intention to spend your day with your mind inclined to see the good everywhere.

You are an observer. You have a body; you experience thoughts and emotions that come and go. You alone remain; you are the witness to all these things.

THERE IS MEANING IN ALL THINGS. BUT ARE YOU PAYING ATTENTION?

Yasmin Mogahed

As you walk from one place to another, become aware of your posture. Notice if you are rushing ahead with your shoulders hunched and carrying tension like a heavy sack. Pull your upper body back and straighten your spine. Be aware of your connection to the ground as each foot is placed one in front of the other. Enjoy being alert and mindful while you walk.

Are you sitting down? Bring your awareness to your chair or the ground and become aware of pressures against your body and textures on your skin. Shift your weight to give you greater comfort and notice any areas of tension such as shoulders, lower back or neck.

LIFE ISN'T HAPPENING TO YOU; LIFE IS RESPONDING TO YOU.

Rhonda Byrne

Appreciate the abundance of wonderful things in your life and give them your attention. Keep a little notebook especially for jotting down memories worth saving, surprises and things you are thankful for.

Wear a piece of jewellery or place stickers on your mobile phone that have significance to you. Whenever you notice them, pause to take in what's happening in your mind and body and be guided towards peace.

Be curious! Open your mind to the new and the unknown in all walks of life.

When you choose to watch a film or listen to some music, notice how powerful the experience can be, when you bring your complete focus and attention to it.

Be a mindful parent, grandparent or godparent by being fully present in your interactions with children. In this way you are helping them to develop a healthy and happy view of themselves.

Welcome all of your feelings. Welcome them like guests and they will leave in their own time.

TRUE MEDITATION IS CONSTANT AWARENESS, CONSTANT PLIABILITY, AND CLEAR DISCERNMENT.

Jiddu Krishnamurti

Allow the telephone to ring three times before you reply, so that you can become aware of your breath and speak from a centred and calm space.

Bring a sense of friendliness to your mistakes. Be gentle and kind to yourself.

IT'S GOOD TO HAVE
AN END IN MIND, BUT
IN THE END WHAT
COUNTS IS HOW
YOU TRAVEL.

Orna Ross

Write down some of your values and ethics to remind you of what you want to prioritise in life. This list can act as a reminder of things to do: spend more time with family, give some money to charity, support a local community project or aim to be more self-sufficient by growing vegetables, etc.

Mindfulness meditation slows down our perception of time, so that short moments appear to be longer. It doesn't give you more hours in your day, but can arouse feelings of spaciousness and calm.

'Let's see' is a useful approach. It allows you to be prepared for anything.

Each moment is your chance to make a choice; embrace life as a young child does, with curiosity, fun and an open heart.

Patience is a much-overlooked quality. It is the ability to remain calm when you may feel provoked. If you have been feeling irritated a lot recently, sit down and contemplate the reasons why. Ask yourself if reacting angrily or impatiently helped the situation. Be kind to yourself and aim to develop a more patient approach.

Notice tiny moments in the day when you can take a breather and realign yourself into the present moment. This could be for a minute before you switch on the television or radio, or close the curtains at night. Be alive to finding such frequent reminders and your days may become more satisfying and composed.

THERE'S NOTHING
SPECIAL ABOUT THE
PRESENT MOMENT
EXCEPT THAT IT'S ALL
WE HAVE.

Dean Sluyter

Live your life saying 'thank you' every day. The more we notice things to appreciate, the more they seem to grow.

If the situation around you is becoming stressful, take some time out away from it and release your tensions. Return with a renewed sense of calm and start afresh.

DO NOT MOVE, DO NOT GO. SINK WITHIN THIS MOMENT. HOLD IT FOREVER.

Virginia Woolf

Take a walk and match your steps to the flow of your breath. Every now and then, stop to look at something such as a tree, a view or a bird. Then continue again with your slow paces mirroring your calm breath. You may only spend ten minutes in this way, yet you may notice far more than you ever have on a walk before.

To be able to empathise with another person's feelings we need to listen to ourselves! Not only must we be aware of their facial, vocal and non-verbal signs, but we need to be alert to and identify our own feelings.

Focus on the person who is talking to you and fully engage in your listening skills.

Sit and bring your presence to the emotion you are feeling right now. Stay still with your senses and acknowledge what it is.

Mindfulness is about paying attention to the things that you find important. Sometimes we need to stop and take stock of how we are spending our time and where we need to make changes. Our personal values and ethical choices not only influence our own lives but have far-reaching consequences.

When you feel pain and sorrow, remember that you have a wounded child within you. Imagine you are cradling that wounded child, caring for her and helping her to heal. Our response to pain is often to bury it deeper and pretend it isn't there. Do the opposite – look within yourself and be mindful of your feelings.

THE ABILITY TO RELAX
AND BE MINDFULLY
PRESENT IN THE
MOMENT COMES
NATURALLY WHEN WE
ARE GRATEFUL.

Joan Borysenko

Remember to say thank you to those people in your life you appreciate.

Relish brief moments of everyday joy instead of lingering on negative events. You will feel happier overall.

THE FUTURE IS ALWAYS BEGINNING NOW.

Mark Strand

In a moment when things are feeling tense, imagine you are holding a dandelion clock. Each seed represents the challenges and discomfort you are experiencing. Release them – blow them away and watch them float, leaving you firmly grounded, strong and calm.

When we say 'My heart isn't in it', we mean that we aren't feeling motivated or joyful over what we are doing. Notice if there are days when you feel like this, and see if you can slow down a little and bring your concentration to the task.

Give your whole attention
to listening to a beautiful
sound; it could be birdsong,
the sea or a piece of
well-loved music.

Get to know *you* – as you
practise mindfulness you
become more aware of
yourself and others.

Before a meeting, project or conversation, take a moment to set your intention. This is a reminder to yourself of the purpose of what you are about to do. It can bring clarity and awareness to your approach.

The mind tends to resort to well-trodden pathways, that is why learning to be mindful takes considerable practice. It is well worth it, in order to break destructive habits and tap in to the flow of deep joy and contentment.

IF YOU PROPOSE TO SPEAK, ALWAYS ASK YOURSELF, IS IT TRUE, IS IT NECESSARY, IS IT KIND.

Buddha

By becoming more mindful
you are also cultivating
your heart. Mind and heart
work together.

Challenges are a gift,
as they can be the teachers
of insight, wisdom
and growth.

FREEDOM IS INSTANTANEOUS THE MOMENT WE ACCEPT THINGS AS THEY ARE.

Karen Maezen Miller

Experience a 'no negativity' day where you look out for both big and small ways to practise gratitude, avoid grumbling and focus on positives with a smile. Acknowledge accomplishments – both yours and others – and be an inspiration to those around you. Repeat again the next day.

As soon as you experience an event you interpret it and give it your own personal meaning. Be aware of this and see how your mind can change things; something that seems negative could contain strands of positive consequences. Look for the positive twist and see how you can turn the world to your advantage.

Your inner wisdom will
reveal itself whenever you
become still, listen to your
heart and trust.

Give your undivided
attention to those you love.

Become more aware of your appetite by listening to the needs of your stomach. Hunger levels vary with the amount of exercise taking place, and are also affected by hormone levels in the body and different seasons of the year. Tune in to your internal cues and become better acquainted with your digestive system.

We all turn to comforting distractions. Sometimes it's worth acknowledging that by letting go of habits nothing terrible happens – you remain alive. The time you would have spent eating junk food, smoking cigarettes, watching hours of television or shopping for more possessions could be swapped for more life enhancing things. Ask yourself what these could be.

AWARENESS IS LIKE
THE SUN. WHEN
IT SHINES ON
THINGS, THEY ARE
TRANSFORMED.

Thích Nhât Hanh

Sharpen your sense of smell. Take notice of the aroma from a flower, a piece of fruit as you bite into it or a warm, revitalising drink.

Every evening with your partner, child, family member or friend, aim to share three good things about your day.

FORGET ABOUT CAPTURING THE MOMENT AND CONCENTRATE ON LIVING IT.

Anonymous

When you walk between rooms or offices, slow your rushing to a calm pace and mentally whisper words or phrases that have a peaceful meaning. This gives you small opportunities to de-stress and take care of yourself throughout the day.

Keep work meetings phone-free, so that everyone attending is completely present. If you have a task to complete, close off all other distractions and train your focus onto the job. Humans have a tendency to be distracted, and the key is to develop the ability to stay concentrating.

Don't underrate yourself.
Value the positive qualities
that you have – and if you
are not sure what they are,
sit down and have a think.

Cultivating mindfulness every day means that you will be more able to deal with difficult events if they arise.

Act on your good ideas and allow the flow of getting started to increase momentum. If you wait until everything is perfect, it may never happen. Be aware that the universe will support you wherever you are right now.

In Sanskrit, early morning is called *brahmamuhurta*, meaning 'the divine time'. Our minds are at their clearest and the air is at its freshest. So early morning is the best time to sit and meditate or contemplate, without distractions from everyday life.

CURIOSITY IS ONE OF
THE GREAT SECRETS
OF HAPPINESS.

Bryant H. McGill

Cultivate a loving heart
so that everything you
encounter can flow easily.

Place candles scented with cedar wood, vanilla or lemon around your home or workplace if suitable. When you catch a little bit of the scent, it can remind you to stay calm and centred.

EVERY MOMENT IS
ENORMOUS, AND IT IS
ALL WE HAVE.

Natalie Goldberg

Sometimes life can become monotonous, so look at your routines to see if they have become robotic. Consider making some changes, even tiny ones, to liven things up.

Humans have over 60,000 thoughts a day. We can't change what we are feeling, but we can alter our reactions to our thoughts. This means becoming conscious of what we are thinking, identifying the thought and realising that it need not dictate our lives. We can observe our thoughts and feelings, let them go and carry on.

The most challenging thing about being mindful is remembering to be mindful.

Be there 100 per cent.

If you're interested in finding out more about our books, find us on Facebook at **Summersdale Publishers** and follow us on Twitter at **@Summersdale**.

www.summersdale.com

Find more mindfulness at
www.placeofserenity.co.uk